WHERE ARE THEY?

By
Anthony Tallarico

kidsbooks®

FIND FREDDIE AROUND THE WORLD

Find Freddie
in the
United
States
and...

- ☐ Alien
- ☐ Barbell
- ☐ Baseball player
- ☐ Beavers (2)
- ☐ Binoculars
- ☐ Carrot
- ☐ Cheese
- ☐ Cook
- ☐ Doctor
- ☐ Dog bone
- ☐ Dogs (2)
- ☐ Elephant
- ☐ Fire hydrant
- ☐ Football player
- ☐ Ice-cream cone
- ☐ Mice (3)
- ☐ Movie camera
- ☐ Octopus
- ☐ Palm trees (4)
- ☐ Rabbits (2)
- ☐ Skier
- ☐ Snake
- ☐ Snowman
- ☐ Stop sign
- ☐ Tent
- ☐ Trash can
- ☐ White House

Find Freddie in this
Winter
Wonderland
and...

- ☐ Balloon
- ☐ Camera
- ☐ Caveman
- ☐ Deer
- ☐ Dogsled
- ☐ Dogs (3)
- ☐ Goose
- ☐ Harpoon
- ☐ Hockey player
- ☐ Ice skates (5)
- ☐ Indian
- ☐ Leprechaun
- ☐ Moose
- ☐ Periscope
- ☐ Police officer
- ☐ Rabbit
- ☐ Raccoon
- ☐ Refrigerator
- ☐ Sailboat
- ☐ Santa Claus
- ☐ Skiers (2)
- ☐ Spear
- ☐ Superhero
- ☐ Telescope
- ☐ Tent
- ☐ Tin man
- ☐ Tree stumps (4)

Find Freddie in the **British Isles** and...

- ☐ Artist
- ☐ Baby carriage
- ☐ Balloon
- ☐ Bicycle
- ☐ Big Ben
- ☐ Bow & arrow
- ☐ Clouds (2)
- ☐ Cow
- ☐ Double-decker bus
- ☐ Ducks (2)
- ☐ Four-leaf clovers (4)
- ☐ Fox
- ☐ Goalpost
- ☐ Golfer
- ☐ Hammock
- ☐ Horse
- ☐ Hot-air balloon
- ☐ Loaf of bread
- ☐ Miners (2)
- ☐ Mouse
- ☐ Mushroom
- ☐ Music notes (4)
- ☐ Pencil
- ☐ Rainbow
- ☐ Scarecrow
- ☐ Scooter

Find Freddie among these Friendly Foreigners and...

- ☐ Anchor
- ☐ Antlers
- ☐ Baby
- ☐ Balloon
- ☐ Barn
- ☐ Bullfighter
- ☐ Camera
- ☐ Cheese
- ☐ Clothespins (4)
- ☐ Deer (2)
- ☐ Eagle scout
- ☐ Eiffel Tower
- ☐ Elephant
- ☐ Fisherman
- ☐ Greek ruins
- ☐ Kite
- ☐ Oil well
- ☐ Owl
- ☐ Panda
- ☐ Picnic basket
- ☐ Pigs (2)
- ☐ Pyramid
- ☐ Rain slicker
- ☐ Telescope
- ☐ Umbrellas (2)
- ☐ Viking
- ☐ Windmill

Find **Freddie** in this
Vast and
Exotic Land
and...

- ☐ Alligators (2)
- ☐ Bigfoot
- ☐ Black bear
- ☐ Bone
- ☐ Camels (2)
- ☐ Duck
- ☐ Elephant
- ☐ Gas pump
- ☐ Lion
- ☐ Magic carpet
- ☐ Mermaid
- ☐ Mongoose
- ☐ Monkey
- ☐ Mount Everest
- ☐ Mount Fuji
- ☐ Music notes (11)
- ☐ Penguin
- ☐ Rhinoceros
- ☐ Sailboats (2)
- ☐ Sheep (2)
- ☐ Snowmen (2)
- ☐ Soccer ball
- ☐ Star
- ☐ Suez Canal
- ☐ Tea bag
- ☐ Umbrella
- ☐ Whale

Find Freddie in this **African Adventure-Land** and...

- ☐ Alligator
- ☐ Ant
- ☐ Banana
- ☐ Bone
- ☐ Cat
- ☐ Crown
- ☐ Diamonds
- ☐ Donkey
- ☐ Egg
- ☐ Fishing nets (2)
- ☐ Fishing pole
- ☐ Flamingo
- ☐ Message in a bottle
- ☐ Moon
- ☐ Mug
- ☐ Mushroom
- ☐ Palm trees (3)
- ☐ Pyramid
- ☐ Rowboats (4)
- ☐ Santa Claus
- ☐ Seal
- ☐ Sunglasses (4)
- ☐ Surfboard
- ☐ Telescope
- ☐ Turtle
- ☐ Zebra

Find Freddie in the Land Down Under and...

- ☐ Apples (6)
- ☐ Barbecue
- ☐ Boot
- ☐ Cloud
- ☐ Cow
- ☐ Crocodile
- ☐ Doctor
- ☐ Eggs (4)
- ☐ Emu
- ☐ Fishing poles (2)
- ☐ Grill
- ☐ Guitar
- ☐ Lifeguard
- ☐ Message in a bottle
- ☐ Octopus
- ☐ Penguin
- ☐ Platypus
- ☐ Sailboats (2)
- ☐ Shark fins (5)
- ☐ Skiers (2)
- ☐ Snake
- ☐ Snowman
- ☐ Surfboards (9)
- ☐ Tasmanian devil
- ☐ Tennis racquets (4)
- ☐ Tire

Find Freddie in this
Blistery Blizzard
and...

- ☐ Airplane
- ☐ Aliens (2)
- ☐ Baseball
- ☐ Box
- ☐ Campfire
- ☐ Circus tents (2)
- ☐ Easel
- ☐ Football
- ☐ Heart
- ☐ Helicopter
- ☐ Ice castle
- ☐ Ice skates (6)
- ☐ Jack-o'-lantern
- ☐ Kangaroo
- ☐ Kite
- ☐ Magic carpet
- ☐ Paintbrush
- ☐ Periscope
- ☐ Santa Claus
- ☐ Skis (4)
- ☐ Sleds (5)
- ☐ Spaceship
- ☐ Stars (2)
- ☐ Tennis racquet
- ☐ Tin man
- ☐ Tombstone
- ☐ Top hats (2)

Find Freddie in South America and...

- ☐ Angel
- ☐ Ant
- ☐ Banana peel
- ☐ Bats (2)
- ☐ Beach ball
- ☐ Beehive
- ☐ Briefcase
- ☐ Candy bar
- ☐ Chinchilla
- ☐ Coconut
- ☐ Condor
- ☐ Dracula
- ☐ Flamingos (2)
- ☐ Iguana
- ☐ Jaguar
- ☐ Manatee
- ☐ Mouse
- ☐ Music notes (3)
- ☐ Ostrich
- ☐ Penguin
- ☐ Pig
- ☐ Shark fins (2)
- ☐ Skull
- ☐ Spider
- ☐ Tires (2)
- ☐ Top hat
- ☐ Toucans (2)

Find Freddie in Central America and...

- ☐ Banana tree
- ☐ Bats (2)
- ☐ Birdbath
- ☐ Bones (2)
- ☐ Broom
- ☐ Bucket
- ☐ Bull
- ☐ Cactus
- ☐ Camera
- ☐ Floating tires (2)
- ☐ Football
- ☐ Golfer
- ☐ Heart
- ☐ Hot-air balloon
- ☐ Kite
- ☐ Pie
- ☐ Piggy bank
- ☐ Pizza
- ☐ Police officer
- ☐ Princess
- ☐ Rabbits (2)
- ☐ Sailboats (4)
- ☐ Snakes (2)
- ☐ Tire
- ☐ Turtle
- ☐ Water skis
- ☐ Whale

Find Freddie
on his
Last Stop
and...

- ☐ Apple
- ☐ Baseball player
- ☐ Beaver
- ☐ Cactus (2)
- ☐ Carrot
- ☐ Cow
- ☐ Cowboys (2)
- ☐ Dogs (3)
- ☐ Trash can
- ☐ Hose
- ☐ Mermaid
- ☐ Octopus
- ☐ Painted egg
- ☐ Paper airplane
- ☐ Parachute
- ☐ Periscope
- ☐ Refrigerator
- ☐ Sailboats (2)
- ☐ Sherlock Holmes
- ☐ Skunk
- ☐ Snowball
- ☐ Suit of armor
- ☐ Tents (2)
- ☐ Whales (2)
- ☐ Witch

Find Freddie and...

Apple	Dish	Hearts (2)	Pencil
Baseball bat	Fire hydrant	Ice-cream cone	Pizza box
Birdcage	Flower	Jump rope	Plate
Bucket	Football helmet	Mitten	Rocking chair
Candle	Frog	Moon	Turtle
Cupcake	Gift	Mouse	

LOOK FOR LISA: TIME TRAVELER

Look for Lisa in
Prehistoric Times
and...

- [ ] Baby carriage
- [ ] Candle
- [ ] Cherry
- [ ] Clothespin
- [ ] Dinosaur egg
- [ ] Faucet
- [ ] Four-leaf clover
- [ ] Hammer
- [ ] Hot chocolate
- [ ] Life preserver
- [ ] Message in a bottle
- [ ] Necklace
- [ ] Necktie
- [ ] "No U Turn"
- [ ] Palm trees (3)
- [ ] Periscope
- [ ] Piggy bank
- [ ] Pizza
- [ ] Skateboard
- [ ] Spool of thread
- [ ] Stars (2)
- [ ] Swimming duck
- [ ] Tire
- [ ] Volcanoes (2)
- [ ] Wooden wheel

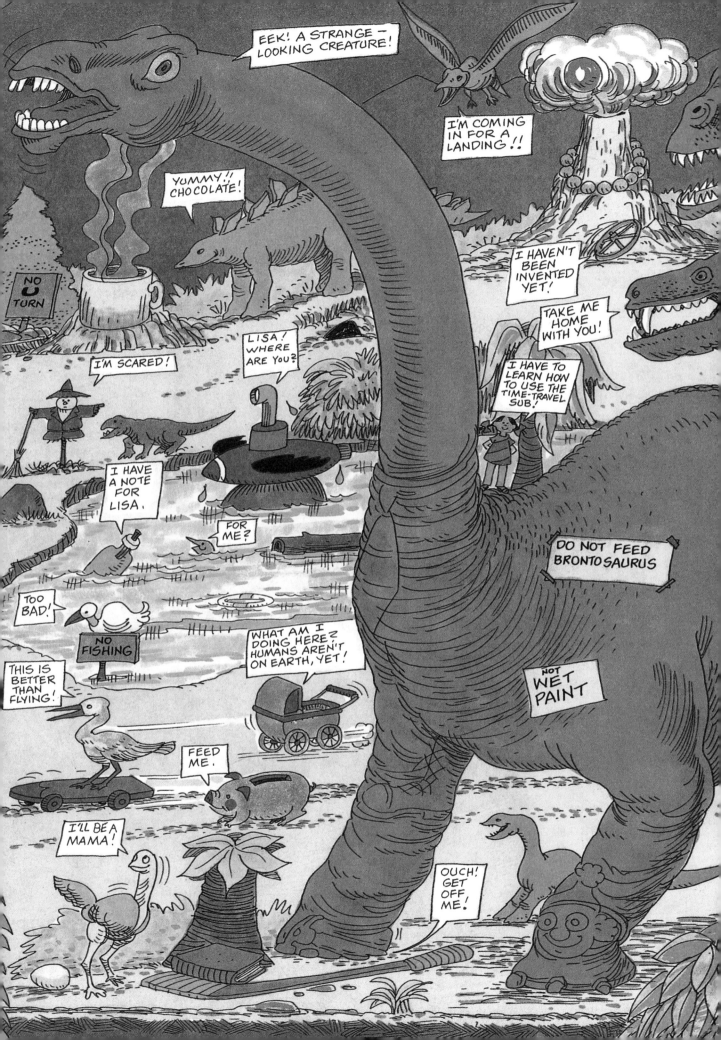

Look for Lisa in the Creepy Castle and...

- ☐ Apples (2)
- ☐ Arrow
- ☐ Ball and chain
- ☐ Balloon
- ☐ Banana peel
- ☐ Baseball cap
- ☐ Birdcage
- ☐ Bones (6)
- ☐ Bowling pin
- ☐ Broom
- ☐ Calendar
- ☐ Carrot
- ☐ Crayon
- ☐ Door knocker
- ☐ Flower
- ☐ Flying bats (3)
- ☐ Football
- ☐ Ghost
- ☐ Jar
- ☐ Lantern
- ☐ Mice (5)
- ☐ Nail
- ☐ Oil can
- ☐ Paintbrush
- ☐ Pencil
- ☐ Rose
- ☐ Scissors
- ☐ Wristwatch

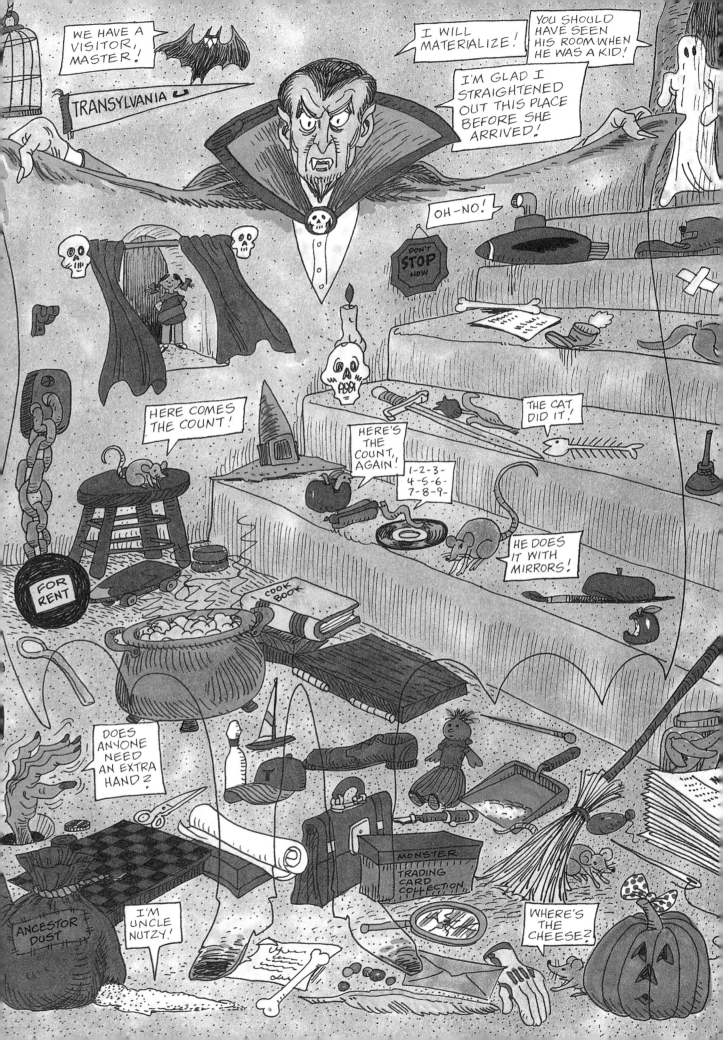

Look for Lisa at this
Historic Happening
and...

- ☐ Antlers
- ☐ Axe
- ☐ Barrel
- ☐ Baseball bat
- ☐ Beach ball
- ☐ Bird
- ☐ Book
- ☐ Bow
- ☐ Bowl
- ☐ Brushes (2)
- ☐ Candle
- ☐ Cat
- ☐ Dog
- ☐ Drums (2)
- ☐ Elephant
- ☐ Eyeglasses
- ☐ Flying bat
- ☐ Hair bows (5)
- ☐ Moon
- ☐ Mouse
- ☐ Pig
- ☐ Pot
- ☐ Puddles (4)
- ☐ Slice of pizza
- ☐ Submarine
- ☐ Surfer
- ☐ Tree stump
- ☐ Wheelbarrow

Look for **Lisa** as she **Rocks and Rolls** and...

Look for Lisa among these Exciting Experiments and...

- ☐ Apple cores (2)
- ☐ Arrow
- ☐ Axe
- ☐ Banana
- ☐ Bell
- ☐ Calendar
- ☐ Cannon
- ☐ Crayon
- ☐ Dart
- ☐ Doctor
- ☐ Fish
- ☐ Football
- ☐ Hamburger
- ☐ Hot-air balloon
- ☐ Jack-in-the-box
- ☐ Medals (2)
- ☐ Nut
- ☐ Piggy bank
- ☐ Puddle
- ☐ Sailboat
- ☐ Sardine can
- ☐ Scarf
- ☐ Shoelace
- ☐ Sock
- ☐ Spool of thread
- ☐ Spoon
- ☐ Totem pole
- ☐ Valentine

Look for Lisa in these
Cavernous Craters
and...

- [ ] Axe
- [ ] Banana
- [ ] Bucket
- [ ] Car
- [ ] Clown
- [ ] Coffee pot
- [ ] Cup
- [ ] Duck
- [ ] Earth
- [ ] Envelope
- [ ] Fish
- [ ] Flashlight
- [ ] Heart
- [ ] Key
- [ ] Kite
- [ ] Ladder
- [ ] Mouse
- [ ] Pig
- [ ] Pumpkin
- [ ] Ring
- [ ] Saw
- [ ] Shovel
- [ ] Stamp
- [ ] Stars (4)
- [ ] Stool
- [ ] Toothbrush
- [ ] Turtle

Look for **Lisa** in the **Ocean** and...

- [ ] Baby
- [ ] Barrel
- [ ] Baseball bat
- [ ] Basketball
- [ ] Boot
- [ ] Bucket
- [ ] Captain's hat
- [ ] Elephant
- [ ] Fish (3)
- [ ] Guitar
- [ ] Heart
- [ ] Homework
- [ ] Hot-air balloon
- [ ] Ice-cream cone
- [ ] Key
- [ ] Oars (5)
- [ ] Painting
- [ ] Palm tree
- [ ] Scuba diver
- [ ] Shark fins (2)
- [ ] Slice of watermelon
- [ ] Sock
- [ ] Surfer
- [ ] Tin can
- [ ] Tire
- [ ] Tree
- [ ] TV set

Look for **Lisa** at this **Special Celebration** and...

- ☐ Axe
- ☐ Barrel
- ☐ Basketball
- ☐ Bear
- ☐ Boat
- ☐ Book
- ☐ Bowling ball
- ☐ Chef
- ☐ Duck
- ☐ Ears of corn (2)
- ☐ Feather
- ☐ Fish
- ☐ Handkerchief
- ☐ Magnifying glass
- ☐ Mouse
- ☐ Owl
- ☐ Paintbrush
- ☐ Pizza delivery
- ☐ Pumpkins (3)
- ☐ Smoke signals
- ☐ Spoon
- ☐ Telephone
- ☐ Tepees (2)
- ☐ Turkeys (2)
- ☐ Turtle
- ☐ Watering can
- ☐ Worm

Look for Lisa at Thomas Edison's Lab and...

- ☐ Bandanas (5)
- ☐ Birdcage
- ☐ Briefcase
- ☐ Cat
- ☐ Chairs (2)
- ☐ Clipboards (2)
- ☐ Club
- ☐ Cookies
- ☐ Cowboy hats (4)
- ☐ Curtains
- ☐ Eyeglasses
- ☐ Film projector
- ☐ Fish
- ☐ Hammer
- ☐ Pail
- ☐ Periscope
- ☐ Picture
- ☐ Plant
- ☐ Rain slicker
- ☐ Roller skates
- ☐ Sailboat
- ☐ Screw
- ☐ Shadow
- ☐ Sheep
- ☐ Trash can
- ☐ Triangle
- ☐ Turtle

Look for Lisa among these **Friendly Aliens** and...

- ☐ Airplane
- ☐ Basketball hoop
- ☐ Briefcase
- ☐ Cactus
- ☐ Crayon
- ☐ Cup
- ☐ Desk lamp
- ☐ Donut
- ☐ Envelope
- ☐ Flower
- ☐ Hamburger
- ☐ Hose
- ☐ Music note
- ☐ "No Parking"
- ☐ Paintbrush
- ☐ Pencils (2)
- ☐ Pirates (2)
- ☐ Pyramid
- ☐ Straw
- ☐ Target
- ☐ Television
- ☐ Top hat
- ☐ Train
- ☐ Trash can
- ☐ Trees (3)
- ☐ Yo-yo

Look for **Lisa** at the **Magic Show** and...

- ☐ Apple
- ☐ Barbell
- ☐ Barrel
- ☐ Beard
- ☐ Box
- ☐ Burned-out lightbulbs (2)
- ☐ Dragon
- ☐ Elephants (2)
- ☐ Football
- ☐ Graduation cap
- ☐ Headband
- ☐ Heart
- ☐ Jack-o'-lantern
- ☐ Key
- ☐ Knight
- ☐ Leaf
- ☐ Mouse
- ☐ Puppy
- ☐ Purple hat
- ☐ Rabbit
- ☐ Sandbag
- ☐ Snake
- ☐ Top hat
- ☐ Weight lifter
- ☐ Trap doors (2)

Look for Lisa and...

Baseball bat	Cane	Moon	Sun
Bird	Fire hydrant	Octopus	Tire
Bottle	Fish	Rabbit	Top hat
Broom	Flowers (2)	Saw	Turtle
Cactus	Hammer	Scarves (2)	Wreath
Can	Kite	Snake	

Search for
Sylvester
at this
Mad Mall
and...

Search for Sylvester in this Fun-Filled Playground and...

Search for **Sylvester** at **Fast Food Heaven** and...

- ☐ Alligator
- ☐ Bat
- ☐ Bone
- ☐ Bowling ball
- ☐ Carrot
- ☐ Club
- ☐ Crowns (2)
- ☐ Dogs (2)
- ☐ Drum
- ☐ Elf
- ☐ Football player
- ☐ Frog
- ☐ Ice-cream cone
- ☐ Jack-o'-lantern
- ☐ Jogger
- ☐ Kite
- ☐ Mouse
- ☐ Owl
- ☐ Pickle
- ☐ Popped balloon
- ☐ Rabbit
- ☐ Shopping bag
- ☐ Skier
- ☐ Snowman
- ☐ Tire
- ☐ Trees (2)
- ☐ Tugboat

Search for **Sylvester** at the **Zany Zoo** and...

- [ ] Baseball bat
- [ ] Baseball caps (4)
- [ ] Bow tie
- [ ] Camel
- [ ] Fish
- [ ] Football
- [ ] Girl with pigtails
- [ ] Kangaroo
- [ ] Little Red Riding Hood
- [ ] Neckties (3)
- [ ] Owl
- [ ] Parrot
- [ ] Pig
- [ ] Pine tree
- [ ] Rabbit
- [ ] Raccoon
- [ ] Scarf
- [ ] School bus
- [ ] Sea horse
- [ ] Seal
- [ ] Shovel
- [ ] Spoon
- [ ] Telescope
- [ ] Top hat
- [ ] Toy turtle
- [ ] Trash can
- [ ] Turtle

Search for Sylvester in this Alphabetical School and...

- ☐ A
- ☐ B
- ☐ C
- ☐ D
- ☐ E
- ☐ F
- ☐ G
- ☐ H
- ☐ I
- ☐ J
- ☐ K
- ☐ L
- ☐ M
- ☐ N
- ☐ O
- ☐ P
- ☐ Q
- ☐ R
- ☐ S
- ☐ T
- ☐ U
- ☐ V
- ☐ W
- ☐ X
- ☐ Y
- ☐ Z

Search for **Sylvester** at the **Basketball Game** and...

- ☐ Alligator
- ☐ Balloons (2)
- ☐ Banana peel
- ☐ Baseball
- ☐ Bowling ball
- ☐ Cannon
- ☐ Cherry
- ☐ Envelopes (2)
- ☐ Eyeglasses (2)
- ☐ Football helmet
- ☐ Ghost
- ☐ Headbands (2)
- ☐ Hot dog
- ☐ Jack-o'-lantern
- ☐ Kangaroo
- ☐ Kite
- ☐ Lost glove
- ☐ Pail
- ☐ Pencil
- ☐ Pizza box
- ☐ Police officer
- ☐ Pom poms (4)
- ☐ Rabbit
- ☐ Snake
- ☐ Stars (3)
- ☐ Tarzan
- ☐ Turtle

Search for Sylvester at this Spooky Mansion and...

Search for
Sylvester
at
Detective
Donald's Digs
and...

- ☐ Broken pencils (3)
- ☐ Calendar
- ☐ Can
- ☐ Candles (3)
- ☐ Chalk
- ☐ Chalkboard
- ☐ Cheese
- ☐ Comb
- ☐ Diploma
- ☐ Fan
- ☐ Fishing pole
- ☐ Hooks (3)
- ☐ Jacket
- ☐ Key
- ☐ Ladder
- ☐ Lamp
- ☐ Medal
- ☐ Nail
- ☐ Paint bucket
- ☐ Screwdriver
- ☐ Shovel
- ☐ Skull
- ☐ Snake
- ☐ Stack of envelopes
- ☐ Sword
- ☐ Tack
- ☐ Top hat

Search for Sylvester at this Silly Circus and...

- ☐ Balloon with star
- ☐ Barrel
- ☐ Cactus
- ☐ Cake
- ☐ Camel
- ☐ Cannon
- ☐ Clothespins (3)
- ☐ Clowns (4)
- ☐ Crayon
- ☐ Firefighter
- ☐ Flowerpot
- ☐ Lightbulb
- ☐ Mice (2)
- ☐ Necktie
- ☐ Party hat
- ☐ Pinocchio
- ☐ Pizza
- ☐ Police officer
- ☐ Skateboard
- ☐ Snowman
- ☐ Spoon
- ☐ Stars (5)
- ☐ Teacup
- ☐ Tin man
- ☐ Unicycle
- ☐ Witch
- ☐ Wizard hat
- ☐ Worm

Search for Sylvester as he Soars Through the Sky and...

- ☐ Banana
- ☐ Baseball bat
- ☐ Bathtub
- ☐ Bird
- ☐ Bow
- ☐ Carrot
- ☐ Cupcake
- ☐ Fishermen (2)
- ☐ Flowers (4)
- ☐ Flying bat
- ☐ Football player
- ☐ Guitar
- ☐ Moon
- ☐ Pot
- ☐ Scarecrow
- ☐ Scarf
- ☐ Shovel
- ☐ Spaceship
- ☐ Stars (3)
- ☐ Sunglasses
- ☐ Target
- ☐ Teapot
- ☐ Tent
- ☐ TV antenna
- ☐ Watering can
- ☐ Witch

Search for Sylvester in Bamboo Town and...

- ☐ Balloons (2)
- ☐ Brooms (2)
- ☐ Drum
- ☐ Eyeglasses (2)
- ☐ Fire hydrants (2)
- ☐ Football
- ☐ Football player
- ☐ Ghost
- ☐ Gift
- ☐ Hard hats (2)
- ☐ Heart
- ☐ Horseshoe
- ☐ Ice-cream cones (2)
- ☐ Jump rope
- ☐ Kangaroo
- ☐ Knight
- ☐ Mask
- ☐ Medal
- ☐ Octopus
- ☐ Pencil
- ☐ Periscope
- ☐ Record
- ☐ Socks (2)
- ☐ Stool
- ☐ Straw
- ☐ Telescope

Search for Sylvester and...

Apple	Carrot	Football	Paintbrush
Bamboo shoot	Cupcake	Horn	Screwdriver
Baseball	Drum	Kite	Spoon
Bone	Fire hydrant	Leaf	Top hat
Candle	Flag	Lock	Turtle
Cane	Flowers (10)	Moon	

WHERE'S WENDY?

Find Wendy at Witchville High School and...

- [ ] Apple
- [ ] Axe
- [ ] Baseball bat
- [ ] Bear
- [ ] Bell
- [ ] Blimp
- [ ] Bowling ball
- [ ] Cauldrons (2)
- [ ] Dog
- [ ] Flying bats (2)
- [ ] Football
- [ ] Green hand
- [ ] Headless man
- [ ] Mask
- [ ] Mushrooms (3)
- [ ] One-eyed monsters (2)
- [ ] Pencil
- [ ] Piece of paper
- [ ] Scarecrow
- [ ] Shovel
- [ ] Skateboard
- [ ] Tire
- [ ] Tombstones (3)
- [ ] Turtle
- [ ] TV antenna
- [ ] Unicorn
- [ ] Walking tree

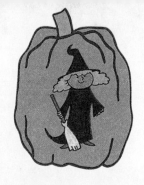

Find Wendy in the
Classroom
and...

- ☐ Baseball bat
- ☐ Bell
- ☐ Bones (2)
- ☐ Books (7)
- ☐ Broken egg
- ☐ Clock
- ☐ Eight ball
- ☐ Eyeglasses (2)
- ☐ Flying bats (2)
- ☐ Football
- ☐ Ice-cream cone
- ☐ Jack-o'-lantern
- ☐ Key
- ☐ Magic wand
- ☐ Needle
- ☐ Octopus
- ☐ Piece of chalk
- ☐ Pizza
- ☐ Rabbit
- ☐ Saw
- ☐ Skeleton
- ☐ Spiders (2)
- ☐ Stool
- ☐ Straw
- ☐ Umbrella

Find Wendy in the
Lunchroom
and...

- [ ] Apple
- [ ] Bird
- [ ] Broken nose
- [ ] Cactus
- [ ] Candle
- [ ] Cat
- [ ] Chick
- [ ] Cookbook
- [ ] Cymbals (2)
- [ ] Drum
- [ ] Flower
- [ ] Football
- [ ] Frying pans (3)
- [ ] Lighthouse
- [ ] Music notes (3)
- [ ] Paper airplane
- [ ] Plate of cookies
- [ ] Santa Claus
- [ ] Skull
- [ ] Snakes (2)
- [ ] Straw
- [ ] Teapot
- [ ] Trash can
- [ ] Turtle
- [ ] Volcano
- [ ] Yellow hand
- [ ] Yellow sock

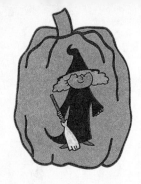

Look for **Wendy** during **Final Exams** and...

- ☐ Ball of yarn
- ☐ Balloon
- ☐ Baseball cap
- ☐ Broken mirror
- ☐ Broken pot
- ☐ Brooms (2)
- ☐ Cheese
- ☐ Chicken
- ☐ Clipboards (4)
- ☐ Cloud
- ☐ Coonskin cap
- ☐ Doctor
- ☐ Duck
- ☐ Elephant
- ☐ Flying bats (3)
- ☐ Football
- ☐ Heart
- ☐ Jack-o'-lantern
- ☐ Lost mitten
- ☐ Magic lamp
- ☐ Mouse
- ☐ Pencil
- ☐ Saw
- ☐ Skulls (2)
- ☐ Stool
- ☐ Tombstone
- ☐ Trunk
- ☐ Worm

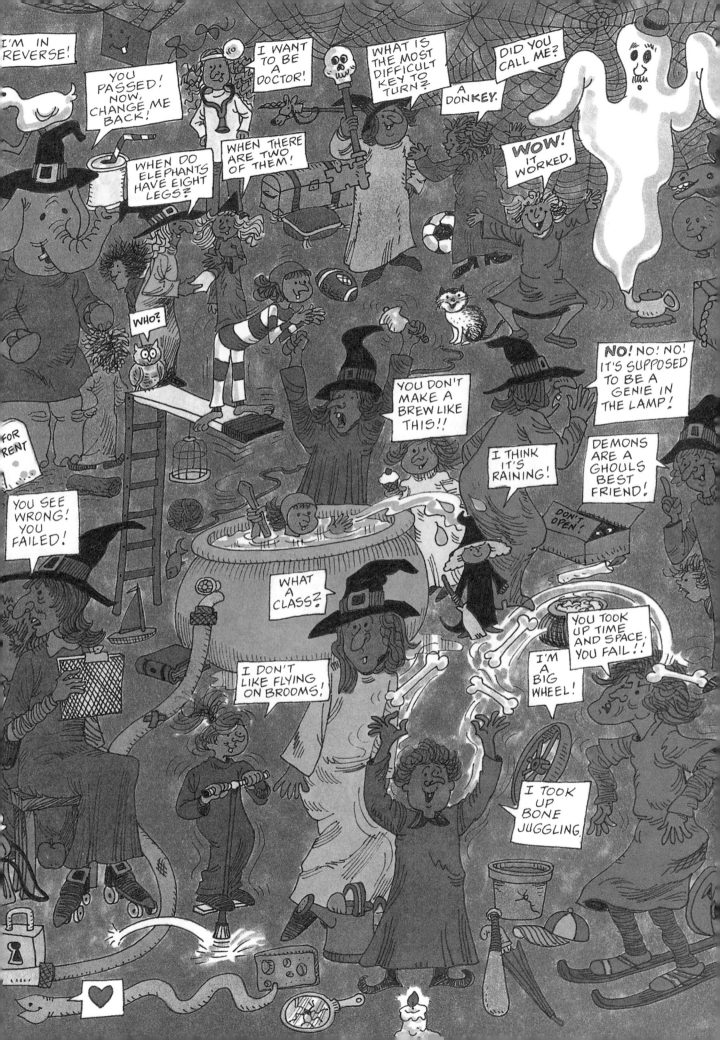

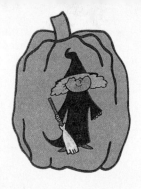

Hunt for Wendy
at
Graduation
and...

- ☐ Barbell
- ☐ Bats (2)
- ☐ Bones (2)
- ☐ Broken mirror
- ☐ Brooms (3)
- ☐ Can
- ☐ Candle
- ☐ Cracked egg
- ☐ Dog
- ☐ Drum
- ☐ Ghost
- ☐ Graduation cap
- ☐ Guitar
- ☐ Hats with horns (2)
- ☐ Kite
- ☐ Marshmallow
- ☐ Moons (2)
- ☐ Music note
- ☐ Sled
- ☐ Target
- ☐ Tire
- ☐ Tombstones (13)
- ☐ Toolbox
- ☐ Umbrella
- ☐ Wizard

Find Wendy in
Count Dracula's Living Room
and...

- ☐ Airplane
- ☐ Baseball bat
- ☐ Birdcage
- ☐ Book
- ☐ Brooms (3)
- ☐ Chair
- ☐ Chicken
- ☐ Cracked egg
- ☐ Crayon
- ☐ Dustpan
- ☐ Mice (3)
- ☐ Mouse hole
- ☐ Mummy
- ☐ Owl
- ☐ Paintbrush
- ☐ Pig
- ☐ Pitcher
- ☐ Spiderweb
- ☐ Teacup
- ☐ Teapot
- ☐ Telephone
- ☐ Top hat
- ☐ Umbrellas (3)
- ☐ Vacuum
- ☐ Worm
- ☐ Wreath

Search for **Wendy** in **Dr. Frankenstein's Laboratory** and...

- ☐ Arrow
- ☐ Ball of yarn
- ☐ Banana
- ☐ Baseball cap
- ☐ Bat
- ☐ Bird
- ☐ Boot
- ☐ Bucket
- ☐ Candles (2)
- ☐ Cheese
- ☐ Clock
- ☐ Eight ball
- ☐ Eyeglasses
- ☐ Flowers (2)
- ☐ Fork
- ☐ Hammer
- ☐ Heart
- ☐ Lips
- ☐ Mask
- ☐ Mice (4)
- ☐ Needle & thread
- ☐ Pig
- ☐ Pizza
- ☐ Present
- ☐ Pumpkin
- ☐ Saw
- ☐ Spoon
- ☐ Stars (4)

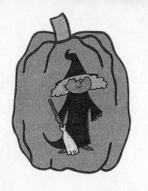

Hunt for Wendy in the
Mummy's Tomb
and...

- ☐ "1st Prize" ribbon
- ☐ Bell
- ☐ Butterfly
- ☐ Cactus
- ☐ Cherry
- ☐ Cracked pot
- ☐ Fire hydrant
- ☐ Fish
- ☐ Giraffe
- ☐ Key
- ☐ Lobster
- ☐ Moon
- ☐ Mouse
- ☐ Painted egg
- ☐ Ring
- ☐ Rooster
- ☐ Sea horse
- ☐ Spiderweb
- ☐ Tepee
- ☐ Top hat
- ☐ Trunk
- ☐ Yellow bird
- ☐ Watering can
- ☐ Winter hat

Find Wendy on the Jack-O'-Lantern Farm and...

Ball of yarn

Bat

Bird

Bucket

Candy cane

Cupid's arrow

Flowers (2)

Hammer

Helmet

Hose

Kite

Pig

Pitchfork

Seal

Worm